Daphne du Maurier Country

Martyn Shallcross

Bossiney Books • Launceston

To Bernice
who introduced me to the world of
Daphne du Maurier – with love

This edition first published 1998 by Bossiney Books,
Langore, Launceston Cornwall PL15 8LD

First published 1987 by Bossiney Books and reprinted 1989, 1990

© 1987, 1998 Martyn Shallcross

ISBN 1 899383 11 5

British Library Cataloguing in publication data:
A CIP catalogue record for this book is available from the British Library.

Acknowledgements

I would like to express my heartfelt thanks to Dame Daphne du Maurier for her help over the years and for opening her private world to me; also to her family, especially Christian Browning, her son, and to members of her household at Kilmarth who always gave me a warm welcome. I would also like to acknowledge the help of Victor Spinetti, Stewart Granger, James Mason, Lady Fitzwilliam, Tamsin Olivier, Joan Fontaine, Donald Sutherland, Val Jones, Judy Ireland, Margaret Fellows, and Mavis and Bill Stubbs and the staff at the Fowey Hotel. Also my mother Essie who first showed me some of Daphne du Maurier country.

Illustration acknowledgements

Photographs are reproduced by kind permission of: Dr Alan Beaumont, page 23; Andrew Besley, page 54; Alice Boyd, page 70; George Ellis, pages 21 and 72; Roy Westlake, front cover (inset) and pages 28, 32, 60 and 87; Judy Ireland (map). Other photographs are from the author's and publisher's own collections.

The inset photograph on the front cover is of Fowey

Origination by Burstwick Print & Publicity Services, Hull.
Printed in Hong Kong by Paramount Printing Ltd., Hong Kong.

Contents

One of the author's extensive collection of photographs of Daphne du Maurier, taken during their twenty year friendship

About the author

Martyn Shallcross knew Daphne du Maurier for over 20 years, during which time he became a close friend of hers. He has since written her biography, *The Private World of Daphne du Maurier*, and has recently completed a play, *Daphne*, which receives its world *première* at the Haymarket Theatre in Basingstoke. The first edition of *Daphne du Maurier Country* was filmed by *The Pebble Mill Chat Show* and later screened as a tribute to Dame Daphne.

He began his writing career by assisting Jesse Lasky Jr and Pat Silver with their biography of Vivien Leigh and Laurence Olivier. He went on to research the best-selling biographies of Merle Oberon and Cary Grant by Charles Higham and Roy Moseley. His show business articles have appeared in several national magazines.

Martyn has also been a regular contributor to television and radio arts programmes, such as *Woman's Hour*, *The John Dunne Show* and *Kaleidoscope*. He has worked for Barry Norman on his 'Hollywood Greats' and weekly film programmes, and enjoyed the opportunity to interview Sophia Loren and Joan Fontaine. Further television appearances have included news and current affairs programmes, such as *Breakfast Time*, *The 9 o'clock News*, *News Night* and a *Book Mark Special* on Daphne du Maurier's novel *Rebecca*.

As a film journalist, Martyn Shallcross has interviewed some of the world's most famous actors and actresses, including Ingrid Bergman and Charlton Heston, Bette Davis, James Mason, Anthony Hopkins, Marlene Dietrich, Stewart Granger and Elizabeth Taylor. One of his most recent interviews was of Julia Ormond about her role in the Hollywood film *First Knight*.

Daphne du Maurier photographed with the author at Kilmarth in 1983. Kilmarth had been her home since 1967

Daphne du Maurier Country

Some locations from the Cornish novels

Kilkhampton

Boscastle

Tintagel

Launceston

Camelford

Altarnun

Jamaica Inn
at Bolventor

R. Tamar

Bodmin

R. Fowey

St Columb

Liskeard

Newquay

Lostwithiel

Castle Dore

Fowey

St Austell • Par

Men-
abilly

Polridmouth
Bay

Plymouth
Sound

Truro

St Ives

Falmouth

Penzance

Helston

Land's End

Helford

French-
man's
Creek

The Loving Spirit
  Polruan, Lanteglos and
  Bodinnick, all opposite Fowey
Jamaica Inn
  Bolventor, Boscastle, Altarnun
Rebecca
  Menabilly, Four Turnings
  (Fowey), Polridmouth Bay

The King's General
  Plymouth Sound,
  Kilkhampton, Falmouth
My Cousin Rachel
  Menabilly, Four Turnings
  (Fowey)
Frenchman's Creek
  Helford and the Helford River

Castle Dor
  Lostwithiel and Castle Dore
House on the Strand
  The area between St Austell
  and the sea
Rule Britannia
  St Austell, Par Beach

Introduction

It is a remarkable fact that some of the most popular novelists in the twentieth century have built international reputations with works infused with Cornish history and drama. Although not born in Cornwall, they have been drawn to the place, lured by its atmosphere and contrasting beauty.

Daphne was born into a wealthy upper-class family in London on 13 May 1907, the second daughter of the celebrated actor, Gerald du Maurier, and his wife, the actress Muriel Beaumont. Her grandfather, George du Maurier, was an artist and caricaturist; his satirical cartoons appeared in the magazine *Punch*, and of his novels, *Trilby* and *Peter Ibbetson* are the best-known.

Gerald du Maurier, Daphne's father, acting with Gladys Cooper and Annie Schletter. He was a highly successful actor-manager and his nonchalant style influenced a whole generation. He was particularly associated with Sir James Barrie, author of Peter Pan

A photograph of Daphne du Maurier, probably taken in the early 1930s around the time her first novel, The Loving Spirit, *was published*

Daphne and her two sisters, Angela and Jeanne, felt smothered by their claustrophobic childhood and often liked to escape London social life; their holidays were invariably spent in Cornwall. When Gerald and Muriel bought 'Ferryside', their holiday home overlooking Fowey Harbour, the love affair between Cornwall and Daphne du Maurier began in earnest.

In the minds of many people, Daphne du Maurier and Cornwall are as synonymous, of course, as Thomas Hardy and Dorset or the Brontë sisters and Yorkshire. She will always be associated with the romance and adventure of this beautiful county which over the years provided her with the inspiration for many of her most successful novels: *Jamaica Inn, The Loving Spirit,*

Frenchman's Creek, *My Cousin Rachel*, *The House on the Strand*, *The King's General* and *Rebecca* (now a publishing legend, with appeal to readers all over the world).

In his book, *The Timeless Land: The Creative Spirit in Cornwall* (Adams & Dart, 1973) Denys Val Baker touched very specifically on the subject of Dame Daphne's relationship with Cornwall – and how she turned that relationship into memorable work:

'Who, for instance, driving over Bodmin Moor and suddenly coming upon the forlorn outline of the now famous Jamaica Inn, at Bolventor, can fail to feel the impact of such a stark, bleak, and out-of-this-world setting? How well, in turn, did Daphne du Maurier capitalise upon this atmosphere in her bestseller *Jamaica Inn*, deepening the shadows, stressing the unease, heightening the general impression of eeriness, of other-worldliness.'

Ferryside, the holiday home first rented and then bought by Gerald du Maurier. Here it is in the 1980s, when Daphne's sister, Angela, lived there

Gerald du Maurier was one of the first 'natural' actors, and became known for wearing his own clothes on stage. He was a famous Captain Hook, Raffles, and many more characters, and made several films in the 1930s

Although a goodly number of Cornish places have become immortalised through the powers of Dame Daphne's descriptive narrative and the sheer readability of her stories, the true locations for many of the scenes in her novels are unknown to the great majority of her readers. The private world of Daphne du Maurier has remained secret for years, the door always locked to outsiders; yet the places that inspired her are often just as stunning as many of her beautifully written passages.

Daphne du Maurier Country re-discovers some of her favourite haunts: a few have been transformed and perhaps today would no longer hold a spell for Daphne; others, like Fowey, are quite timeless and remain as attractive as they always were.

Daphne's career began and ended in the county that triggered the creation of some of her greatest work. She died peacefully in her sleep in 1989, but with each passing year fascination in this extraordinary novelist has continued to grow. With a festival named after her, and plays and television series appearing with regularity, I am sure she would have been pleased by such increasing enthusiasm for her work. I would like to think that somewhere she is looking down benevolently at all the interest in her remarkable life.

Fowey from Polruan

What makes one person able to evoke love and affection for an individual novel or its film adaptation is a difficult question to answer; perhaps it is a particular way of smiling, an interesting lilt of the voice during some spoken dialogue or a richness of words on the printed page. If you place all these idiosyncrasies together they produce a magical essence that you remember over the years. Everyone is special, but perhaps some people are more gifted than others, either with original and rare beauty or with

One of Daphne du Maurier's favourite views, towards Polridmouth Beach. Cornwall's coastal weather is always changing, creating endless variety and haunting moodiness. She said 'It is so lovely, even in the rain. I would rather be out walking on the beach and headland than anything else I come to think of'

incomparable intellect. For anyone to create affection and love from just a few novels, as Daphne du Maurier has done, is in itself something exceptional.

The passage of time is often swift and our memory of the past can sometimes be overlooked and forgotten. But somehow a period or epoch can remain unchanged in our mind forever, and be brought to our consciousness by a certain event, maybe a dash of colour, a line of dialogue, a shadow, a sigh, a smile, a memory. These memories, whether illusory, imagined or true, should be treasured as a wonderful reminder of a golden age. The curiosity about Daphne du Maurier will never die as long as love and memories last; she will continue to inspire and excite people in the county she made her own. This book is my own affectionate tribute to a friend I knew for over 20 years.

Martyn Shallcross 1998

Cornwall and the Loving Spirit

> Alas – the countless links are strong
> That bind us to our clay.
> The loving spirit lingers long
> And would not pass away.

> Emily Brontë

The reason why Cornwall exerts such a hold on so many may be due to a combination of factors: it has a long history and people with a language of their own; it also has ancient customs, superstition and legends, as well as magnificent scenery on the coast and inland. These all blend together to create a unique and memorable county.

The real genesis of Daphne du Maurier's love affair with Cornwall probably began in her childhood when, as a five-year-old little girl, she came to Mullion Cove on the Lizard Peninsula, and then five years later to Kennack Sands, also on the Lizard Peninsula.

Like many other city families, the du Mauriers regularly took their holidays in Cornwall. No doubt the beautiful beaches, the coastline and the recreational activities would all have contributed to the fascination experienced by the young Daphne and her family when they first visited. Daphne, in particular, began to discover the area around Fowey and its magic drew her back again and again. The picturesque harbour, with its ships going about their daily business, appealed to her, and the stories of the local people were stored away in her subconscious, later to be recalled and to set fire to her imagination.

Cornwall has always attracted the Bohemian like a magnet and this, too, may have been a factor for Daphne: the daughter of actor-manager Sir Gerald du Maurier and the grand-daughter of George du Maurier, famous for *Trilby*, she was exposed from an

For Daphne du Maurier as for so many others, her first experience of Cornwall was from childhood holidays, and her love affair with Cornwall began then and never faded

Opposite: Cadgwith, a beautiful and still unspoilt fishing village near Kennack Sands on the Lizard

Right: The sands at Kynance

early age to writers, actors and creative personalities. Jesse Lasky, Jr, son of the famous film pioneer, remembers one visit to the du Mauriers at Cannon Hall in Hampstead: 'In those days, before her marriage, Daphne was a real Bohemian, reading poetry and acting rather unconventionally.'

We can imagine the contrast between the sophistication and excitement of social Hampstead and the tranquil pleasures of Fowey.

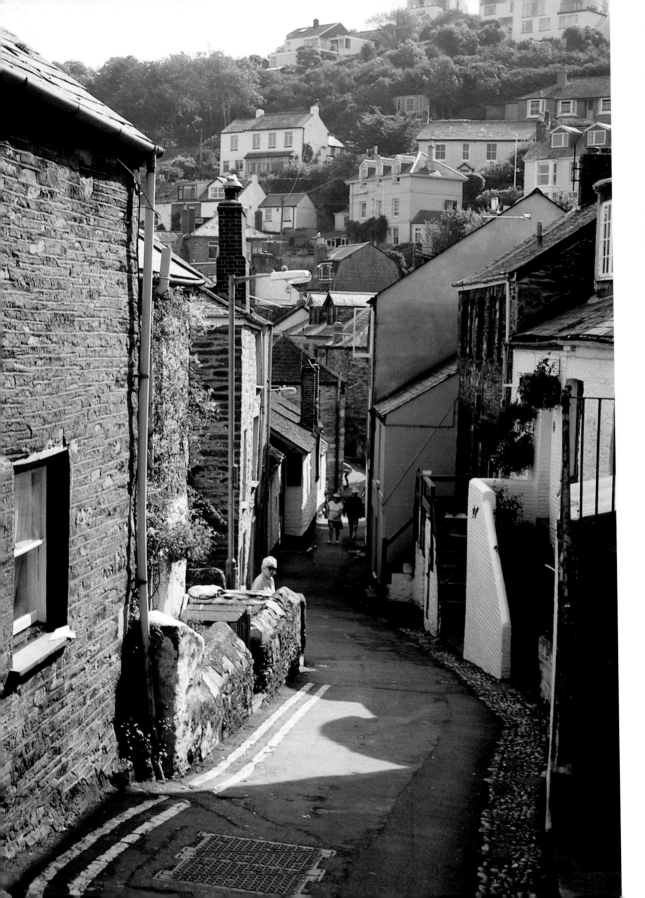

Opposite: a street in Polruan – 'Plyn' in The Loving Spirit *– whose clustered cottages and narrow streets fascinated Daphne from an early age. Above: The boatyard in the story still exists today*

The du Mauriers usually rented houses, but the house which especially won their hearts was a Swiss-type cottage near the ferry at Bodinnick. After renting it for a period the family bought Ferryside, and it was here that Daphne began her very first novel *The Loving Spirit*. Gazing across the harbour, Daphne was captivated by the view – all of which helped her to conceive the story of the fictional family.

The story was to revolve around the village of 'Plyn': this was actually Polruan, and the boat-building family originated from the boatyard, also in Polruan. Using and describing local places in her narrative has immortalised the area around Fowey.

Here fact and fiction merged. Like the hero and heroine of The Loving Spirit, *Daphne and her husband 'Boy' Browning travelled to their wedding by boat, landing here at Pont...*

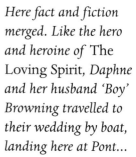

... and walking up the woodland path to the lovely and isolated church of Lanteglos

In later life Daphne would often visit Pont Pill ('pill' is the local word for a creek) to see fellow author Leo Walmsley in his army hut

From the windows of Ferryside Daphne was to have her first sight of her future husband when he sailed round Fowey harbour in his white motor boat. Angela du Maurier remarked, 'He looks interesting!' 'Boy' Browning had originally travelled to Cornwall after reading *The Loving Spirit* and being intrigued by the writer and location of the novel. After an initial meeting a courtship developed, and they were soon married. Like the young couple in *The Loving Spirit*, they went by boat to Lanteglos Church for their wedding. Daphne told me: 'All I did on my honeymoon was to go up the Helford River to Frenchman's Creek.'

Daphne used to like to take people to visit this grave in Lanteglos church-yard, that of Jane Slade (Janet Combe in the novel) which was one of the inspirations for The Loving Spirit

We find this curious intermingling of fact and fiction running through Dame Daphne's life. *The Birds*, for example, so success-ful as a film for the big screen, directed by the legendary Hitchcock, really owed its genesis to Cornwall: 'I got the idea for the story of *The Birds* from watching the seagulls chase the farmer's tractor at Menabilly Barton. Also, below the farm many gulls gather after storms. One afternoon as I walked down to P'ridmouth, the gulls flew straight after me and my dog. This is how I got the idea of birds attacking people.'

The Brontë sisters may have been born and brought up in Yorkshire, but they had a Cornish mother, Maria Branwell, who came from Penzance. Their novels, including *Jane Eyre* and *Wuthering Heights*, became literary landmarks. To what extent Daphne's writing style was influenced by the Brontë sisters is open to debate. What we can say for certain is that her first novel, *The Loving Spirit*, was inspired in title alone from a haunting poem written by Emily Brontë.

There is a further parallel in that both sisters, like Daphne du Maurier, merged personal experience with imagination, and became closely associated with an area – in their case the towns and moors of Yorkshire. It is interesting to note that Daphne's association with Cornwall was highlighted in her book *Vanishing Cornwall*: one might almost call it a Cornish autobiography, and in it she devotes a whole chapter to the Brontë family and their Cornish connections.

It was in 1960 that Daphne du Maurier's *The Infernal World of Branwell Brontë* appeared, published by Victor Gollancz. In it she turned her literary and historical searchlights on to this short-lived but highly talented family who lived in Haworth Parsonage where manuscripts running to many hundreds of thousands of words were penned inside its four walls.

Branwell Brontë's work may not have had quite the same polish and power as his famous sisters', but his was a boyhood and youth of staggering productivity. His flame flickered early – brilliantly – so much so that the lives and loves of his imaginary characters became part of a burning-out process and, by the age of twenty-one, his invention was exhausted. Branwell's was indeed an 'infernal world': 'haunted by demons', seeing 'luminous substances in his imagination' and suffering 'frequent trembling of the limbs'. He died on a Sunday morning in 1848, at the age of only thirty-one.

His biographer took the view that he was more likely to have been suffering from fits rather than delirium tremens, a condition triggered by alcohol. Her careful research and writing led to a portrayal of a sad figure, ultimately unloved, in a contented household: a curious castaway (at the very outset of the book, there are lines quoted from William Cowper's 'The Castaway').

In one of my meetings with Daphne she told me, 'I nearly drank some laudanum like Branwell, but I gave up and poured it down the sink.'

Cornwall's past has been beautifully recalled in many of the books of Daphne du Maurier. The historical novel is one of the most difficult literary genres. There is a certain limiting effect; there is the need to adhere to a particular pattern – a pattern

A portrait of Lady du Maurier, mother of Daphne and her two sisters, Angela and Jeanne. It was taken on 5 August 1946 by George Ellis

defined by history which demands a marked degree of accuracy. 'It's a difficult business,' she once admitted. 'The fact is I've always been interested in the past. The real problem is striking a balance. You've lots of truth to go on, and yet you want to hold the attention of your reader. You play about with things a bit, but it's a little tricky ... you hate to go wrong with basic history. The older I get, the keener I get on truth. Naturally though I take liberties with dialogue ... the historical novelist must.'

Getting to the question 'Why Cornwall?', when asked this once Dame Daphne replied: 'It is still so lovely even in the rain. I would rather be out walking on the beach and headland, and looking out at my Cornwall, than anything else I come to think of.' Even at the age of eighty the magic of Cornwall still held a spell over her.

The versatile du Maurier

Last night the other world came much too near.
And with it fear...

'Another World', *The Rebecca Notebook*

It was in 1934 that Daphne really broke into the headlines with a biography of her father, Sir Gerald du Maurier. The candour of that biography apparently upset some people, but Sir Gerald's daughter had no regrets: 'Father always said, "You've got to tell the truth," and I wrote the book as he would have written it ... at least, that's how I see it.'

Despite her theatre background, the young Daphne had no desire to go on the stage: 'I enjoyed watching my father act. I

Daphne in 1976. Gerald's statue stands on the sill, watching over her

thought him wonderful, but the theatre didn't appeal to me personally. In fact, going backstage after a show, when people came round with their congratulations, I found it all most embarrassing.' (Daphne did, of course, later write for the theatre – *The Years Between*, *September Tide* and an adaptation of her bestselling *Rebecca*.)

The range of du Maurier writing is extensive. It includes one volume of autobiography, *Growing Pains*, five biographies, a baker's dozen of novels, five volumes of short stories, one travel publication, *Vanishing Cornwall*, two plays and then in 1981 *The Rebecca Notebook and Other Memories*. This last book fascinatingly reveals how Rebecca came to be written, its origin and development. The memories section is partly autobiographical and to some extent about her beliefs. Readers also encounter her distinguished grandfather, George du Maurier, whose *Punch* illustrations made him a

The genesis of Daphne du Maurier's short story The Birds *was here in Cornwall: a flock of gulls flew aggressively after Daphne while she walked along the beach at Polridmouth, because they were starving.*

Daphne du Maurier's imagination, and her gift for dragging up those irrational fears that lurk inside so many of us, worked on this personal adventure to make something special – as Hitchcock immediately recognised

"It could be the most terrifying motion picture I have ever made!"—

"...and remember, the next scream you hear may be your own!"

ALFRED HITCHCOCK'S "The Birds"

TECHNICOLOR®

ROD TAYLOR · JESSICA TANDY
SUZANNE PLESHETTE and Introducing 'TIPPI' HEDREN

Based on Daphne Du Maurier's Classic Suspense Story

A Fascinating

The poster for Hitchcock's adaptation of The Birds *in 1963. Daphne's location for the story was changed, and filming took place in North California. The end results pleased her very much*

famous figure; and her father, Gerald, for whom Sir James Barrie wrote *Peter Pan*. Her writing in this section also ranges across such subjects as romantic love and widowhood, religion and success – and death.

Today it is perhaps not easy for younger generations to understand that in her heyday Dame Daphne won golden approval all over the world. *Time and Tide* reviewing her novel *The Scapegoat*, first published by Gollancz in 1957, wrote: 'From the original beginning to the inevitable end this book is one of her best.'

Here is Ronald Bryden writing in *The Spectator* in April 1962:

'Penguin Books have recognised, by giving her the full regal reprinting previously awarded Lawrence, Graham Greene and Evelyn Waugh, that Miss du Maurier is one of the world's great literary phenomena. It is about time somebody did. Miss du Maurier's novels have been read by millions of people in scores of languages. The films made from them have been seen by millions more. In France, her works rank with Durrell's and Charles Morgan's; in the US they are automatic book-club choices. Largely by her efforts, Britain still leads the world in romantic fiction.'

Hitchcock, in the words of Daphne du Maurier, was 'famous for his treatment' of her work. He filmed three of her stories, which was most unusual

However, an *Observer* critic reviewing *The Birds* said: 'Anyone starting this book under the impression that he may sleepily relax is in for a shock ... continually provokes both pity and terror.'

Such words completely demolish the idea that she was purely and simply a romantic novelist.

Critics on the other side of the Atlantic invariably gave Daphne a good press: *The New York Times* once referred to her as 'in a class by herself', and *McCall's* called her 'a master of suspense', while *Chicago Tribune Book World* said: 'Daphne du Maurier sweeps dust away and brings her stories alive. It is a rare talent ... In this century few English-speaking authors seem to keep that particular magic. Somerset Maugham was one, and du Maurier is most definitely another.'

After being locked in a cage which the birds were persuaded to attack, Tippi Hedren felt Hitchcock was sadistic in his search for realism

Jamaica Inn

'There's things happen at Jamaica Inn, Mary, that I've never dared to breathe. Bad things. Evil Things. I dare not even admit them to myself.'

Jamaica Inn was first published in January 1936. In those days the inn was a temperance house on the twisting, turning moorland road linking Bodmin and Launceston. But in her imagination Daphne du Maurier saw it in the 1700s. Although genuine place names figure in the pages, in her note at the beginning of the novel the author says, 'Characters and events described are entirely imaginary.'

The heroine is recently-orphaned Mary Yelland who leaves her home at idyllic Helford to go and live with her aunt at Jamaica Inn, Bolventor. Mary is horrified to find that her once pretty Aunt Patience has become a shadow of herself – living under the influence of her husband Joss Merlyn, a bully of a man who is engaged in smuggling and murder.

Jamaica Inn as it is today

Desolate and majestic Bodmin Moor: Brown Willy as seen from Rough Tor

The old inn sign at Jamaica Inn

Like the novel *Rebecca*, this story deals with a young girl alone in the world, cast adrift in an unfamiliar, hostile environment. Daphne du Maurier's descriptions of the moor are undoubtedly some of the finest in any Cornish novel. Here, too, she builds up an impressive portrait of Cornwall in the 1700s; at a deeper level we sense the loneliness of the moor and the feeling of fear and isolation that Mary Yelland must have experienced.

Throughout this tale many of the characters are loathsome – and elicit no sympathy from the reader – and her superlative story-telling enables us to share the predicament in which Mary Yelland finds herself. Sent to bed by her Uncle Joss, Mary hears strange sounds and, through a crack in her blind, she sees strange

Above: The former vicarage at Altarnun, now a hotel
Opposite: a scene from the 1939 film, as Mary Yelland is left to her fate at
Jamaica Inn. Daphne thought Maureen O'Hara was wonderful as Mary

bundles being carried to and fro. One cannot help remembering the refrain from Rudyard Kipling's 'A smuggler's song':

> Them that asks no questions isn't told a lie.
> Watch the wall, my darling, while the gentlemen go by!

Daphne herself visited Bolventor in the 1930s. She told me, 'I got the idea for the novel *Jamaica Inn* during an expedition with my friend Foy Quiller-Couch when we visited Jamaica Inn on horseback. During the evening I began to read *Treasure Island* and that is when the characters began to develop and the idea of *Jamaica Inn*, with wrecking and smuggling, became clear to me. My meeting with the parson from Altarnun helped me formulate the story and somehow the characters began to develop in my subconscious and I clearly imagined the vicar in a more sinister role.'

Dozmary Pool, one of the loveliest features of Bodmin Moor, appears in Jamaica Inn

It was mid-November and during the day Daphne and Foy visited some of the well-known spots nearby, including Dozmary Pool and the church at Altarnun. At Altarnun they had made friends with the local parson and during the evening he came to visit both girls at Jamaica Inn where they talked long into the night by a large warm peat fire. All of this helped to fuel Daphne's imagination as the tale began to form in her mind.

When the book was published it was a great popular success and the film rights were soon sold to Charles Laughton and Eric Pommer. Before leaving for America Alfred Hitchcock had rather rashly agreed to film *Jamaica Inn* – he had been friendly with Sir Gerald du Maurier and, though claiming no special affection for her work, he went on to film three du Maurier novels. Indeed, over the years Hitchcock became famous for his treatment of du Maurier's work. (Laughton and Hitchcock had a good deal in common: they were exactly the same age and both were large men who came from comfortable middle-class backgrounds.)

However, Hitchcock quickly realised that *Jamaica Inn* 'was an absurd thing to undertake'. Setting up the production was thwart with problems and the screenplay was rewritten by Sidney Gilliat, Daphne having declined the opportunity.

At Charles Laughton's request, JB Priestley was brought in to specifically build up the squire's role. Hitchcock felt the novel's one redeeming feature was that it was a whodunnit. The landlord

Altarnun is a sprawling parish, at over 15,000 acres the biggest in Cornwall. In Daphne's story, the vicar of Altarnun must surely be the most enigmatic and evil of all her characters

1939 poster for Hitchcock's film, Jamaica Inn. *Daphne only really enjoyed the wrecking scene*

was obviously only a henchman, whereas the head of the smugglers was a man of substance. In the novel this was the parson, but Laughton had the story changed to avoid the wrath of the film censors who would not have passed a man of the cloth being depicted as evil. In his new role as squire, he replaced the parson as leader of the smugglers. With this change, however, much of the power of the original novel was lost.

Of the film Daphne du Maurier said: 'I was not consulted. I thought the wrecking scene at the beginning good, but I think they could have done a lot more with the story. In fact, they changed the theme and this affected the plot.' Because of the changes in both the characters and plot, it would seem Hitchcock tackled the film lackadaisically; there were also rumours that Hitchcock and Laughton fell out during the production.

The exhilarating north coast of Cornwall, where the wrecking scenes in Jamaica Inn are set. This photograph is of the celebrated Bedruthan Steps

Trevor Eve and Jane Seymour in the 1983 adaptation of Jamaica Inn. *The novels continue to present a challenge to film-makers today*

For all its faults *Jamaica Inn*, made in 1939, had a star-studded cast, including Charles Laughton, Leslie Banks, Emlyn Williams, Robert Newton and Maureen O'Hara. This film gave Maureen O'Hara her first major role, but Hitchcock's relationship with her was distant and as usual he was more interested in the mechanics of film-making than looking after the performances of individual actors.

On release *Jamaica Inn* was a considerable box office success, enhancing du Maurier's reputation and paving the way in the United States for her considerable popularity as an author.

Rebecca

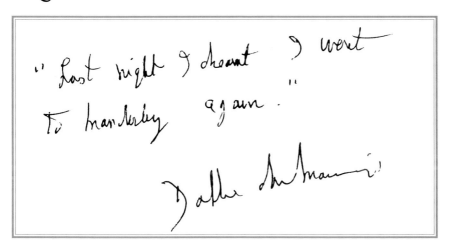

"Last night I dreamt I went to Manderley again."

Daphne du Maurier

Rebecca is one of the great bestsellers in the history of publishing, and is read and enjoyed in many languages. It has been outstanding in five ways: as a novel, as a film, as a play, as a television series and even as an opera. First published in 1938 it was an immediate success both in Britain and in North America.

In Britain alone during its first year of publication millions of people took it to heart, identifying strongly with the predicament of the nameless heroine for ever shadowed by the menacing ghostly presence of the dead Rebecca.

The story of *Rebecca* could be likened to classical tales such as *Cinderella* and *Jane Eyre* – a fact confirmed in an early line of Jack Favell to Mrs Danvers: 'Careful Danny, we don't want to shock Cinderella, do we?' From her first appearance, the housekeeper, Mrs Danvers, could almost be thought of as one of the ugly sisters and Jack Favell as an ally of hers.

Rebecca concerns itself with the story of a gauche young girl who meets sophisticated and mysterious Mr Maxim de Winter holidaying on the French Riviera. Maxim is seemingly there to recover from the death of his beautiful wife, Rebecca, while the nameless heroine is the companion of the odious and vulgar Mrs van Hopper. A whirlwind romance develops; Maxim marries the

Milton House, near Peterborough: some of its rooms, with their long mullioned windows and window seats, remembered from her childhood, were used by Daphne for the interior scenes of Manderley

One of Daphne's personal photographs of Menabilly, neglected and thickly clad with ivy, before she took it on a long-term lease in 1943. She subsequently totally transformed the place. Menabilly was used for the setting of many of the scenes in Rebecca

girl and they return to his family home, Manderley, in Cornwall. Here, the nervous young girl, suddenly elevated to the status of mistress of the household, finds herself confronted by the sinister Mrs Danvers, the housekeeper who adored Rebecca. As time goes on, she becomes terrified by Mrs Danvers who keeps the rooms where Rebecca lived exactly as they were when she was alive – especially Rebecca's bedroom in the west wing.

When walking round the grounds of Manderley, the young girl discovers the beach house where Rebecca once entertained her friends. It would be here later that Maxim would tell her how he killed Rebecca and why he did not love her.

Preparing for a ball at Manderley, Mrs Danvers advises her to wear a dress copied from one of the family portraits. Unwittingly she therefore wears the same dress that Rebecca had worn. When Maxim sees his second wife thus dressed he becomes furious. During the party a boat is wrecked in the bay. Divers go down and another boat is found – Rebecca's, her body still inside. An inquest is demanded. Maxim now has to explain how and why he identified another woman's body as his wife Rebecca. Through Mrs Danvers, Maxim and his second wife find the name of Rebecca's doctor in London. They eventually track down the doctor who explains that Rebecca actually did not have long to live, as she had cancer. A verdict of suicide is therefore given.

The beach-house at Polridmouth features in the novel as Rebecca's cottage where she was murdered

A general view south past the Beach House, across Polridmouth Bay towards the Gribbin

Jack Favell rings Mrs Danvers at Manderley and tells her the news. The housekeeper goes insane and sets fire to the house. As Maxim drives westward back to Manderley, he sees the crimson sky.

In terms of construction *Rebecca* is another fascinating mixture of fact and fiction. Manderley, which is a central plank of the whole story, is a combination of two real houses: Menabilly, hard by Fowey, and Milton, near Peterborough. The author had, in fact, visited Milton twice in her childhood and the place must have made a tremendous impression – for the memory of those two visits stayed with her all her life. She used some of the rooms and several portraits to describe the interior of her fictional house. Daphne told me: 'The entrance hall at Milton was exactly as I described in *Rebecca*, when the second wife arrives for the first time at Manderley, and meets the household staff – the only difference being that I described a sweeping staircase coming down into a hallway.'

The whole atmosphere of Milton during Daphne's visits would have been very formal and correct: a full house staff of butler,

The author by the wreck on Polridmouth beach. During the 1930s, Daphne witnessed the wrecking of this boat on the beach and it later gave her the idea of using a wreck in her story

housekeeper, cook and housemaids. It is interesting to reflect that in *Rebecca* the housekeeper plays such an important, significant part. Daphne had this to say about her: 'I had seen the black dress and the chain with keys on a housekeeper in one of the houses I stayed at. It could have been Milton or another house. The rest of the description is imaginary.' During 1917 the housekeeper at Milton was a Miss Parker, who was described as 'tall, dark and very commanding'. She could indeed have prompted the idea for Mrs Danvers.

The setting for the novel *Rebecca* is largely the grounds around what was to become Daphne's home, Menabilly, near Fowey, including the beach house. Polridmouth Bay is also the scene for Rebecca's murder and the wreck of her boat.

Daphne and her sister Angela first discovered Menabilly's grounds in the late 1920s during a summer expedition walking

This gateway, beside the Four Turnings roundabout above Fowey, was the entrance to the old drive to Menabilly, which used to be overgrown and impassable. It was this drive which was remembered by Daphne at the start of Rebecca *when she was moved to write that magnificent opening sentence 'Last night I dreamt I went to Manderley again'*

around the coastline near Fowey, but they found that to get to the house they needed to walk down an overgrown drive about three miles long – the entrance being at the crossroads at Four Turnings. It was this journey along the drive, twisting and turning and apparently impassable, that Daphne was to describe in the poignant beginning to her novel when she wrote the now famous words, 'Last night I dreamt I went to Manderley again.'

On another visit to Fowey, Daphne finally got to Menabilly properly. She found, at long last, her mysterious house of secrets which was not only an inspiration for *Rebecca* but was also woven into her other Cornish novels: *My Cousin Rachel, The King's General* and *Frenchman's Creek.*

When driving me back to my hotel in Fowey, Daphne once told me all about the drive at the beginning of *Rebecca*. As we came to Four Turnings she said: 'That is the drive I had in mind when I wrote *Rebecca*, you know "Last night I dreamt..."'

After this discovery of Menabilly, which in those days was neglected and covered in ivy, Daphne would often, in her own words, 'trespass' in the grounds for hours at a time. Then she wrote to the owners asking for permission to trespass in the woods around the house and they generously gave their consent. Eventually the owners allowed her to take on a long-term lease of the property, and residence at Menabilly began in 1943. It was to last for twenty-four years, ending in a move to Kilmarth in 1967.

When she first lived at Menabilly everyone thought she was mad because the house was neglected and run-down, but after a few months the ivy was removed, the roof repaired and life appeared in the building once again. Daphne lived here with her husband, Boy Browning, and their children, two girls and a boy. Although she was now married with a growing family to care for,

Polkerris, at the heart of du Maurier country, is a small half-moon cove in a wide amphitheatre of hills. The Rashleigh Inn is named after the family which Daphne often featured in her work. In Rebecca, Polkerris was 'Kerrith'

Menabilly, in about 1983. The Manderley of Rebecca was largely this apparently secret house, tucked away in romantic Cornish woodlands within the sound of the sea

Daphne's imagination was not dampened or her enthusiasm for writing diminished. She had placed a small summer house in the grounds in which to work.

Daphne at Menabilly in the late 1940s with her elder daughter Tessa on her right, her son Christian and younger daughter Flavia on her left

It was, of course, more than the house that fascinated her: there was the history of the Rashleigh family who, for generations, had occupied Menabilly – and who were destined to appear again and again in her novels in one disguise or another. Then there were the Quiller-Couches who told Daphne about one member of the Rashleigh family who had been married first to a very beautiful wife, whom he had divorced, and then he married a very much younger woman. Ideas began to develop in Daphne's imagination. There had also been a wreck in the bay at Polridmouth – and down on the shore was a beach or boathouse. So the basic story began to germinate.

Some years later and after her marriage, Daphne was stationed with her husband in Alexandria, Egypt, and she began to feel homesick. Her obsession with Menabilly began to surface in both her thoughts and her writing, and it was here in Egypt that she started writing *Rebecca*, remembering her beloved Cornwall – and maybe distance and longing sharpened her memory and imagery.

Lobby card for the film of
Rebecca *in 1940*

The famous balcony scene in Rebecca, with Joan Fontaine and Judith Anderson

Returning to England, the Brownings were stationed at Aldershot where they rented a house called Greyfriars, near Fleet. Here Daphne completed the novel. She told me: 'I began the novel in the first person and I avoided giving the heroine a name because it became an interesting exercise in writing and technique.'

Upon publication, the novel became an instant success in Britain and in North America. Serialised in the newspapers, it whetted readers' appetites, and the radio *première* of the story, produced by Orson Welles (who also starred in the production in December 1938) made a listening public keen to see the film version. The film rights were sold to David Selznick by Daphne's agent, Curtis Brown, and it was announced that Alfred Hitchcock would direct. Laurence, now Lord Olivier, would star alongside a newcomer, Joan Fontaine, who was Olivia de Havilland's sister. The rest of the cast included Daphne's old friend Gladys Cooper as Bea, Judith Anderson as Mrs Danvers and George Sanders as Jack Favell.

This time Hitchcock followed the story faithfully, careful to retain the fairy tale elements. He also did not want to lose the quintessential Englishness of the novel which made *Rebecca* so attractive. The film is Hitchcock at his most masterly: though he had some reservations about it, it stands as a supreme example of his craft. Moreover its success all over the world confirmed Daphne du Maurier's place among the popular authors of the twentieth century.

French poster advertising the 1940 Hitchcock film of Rebecca *which Daphne greatly admired*

Joan Fontaine's personal photograph of herself in her role as the second Mrs de Winter, for which she received an Oscar nomination

The film won an Oscar for the Best Film and there was an Oscar nomination for Joan Fontaine.

Joan Fontaine told me: 'During the filming of *Rebecca* there was tension and I did feel just like that little nobody in the story, but this helped me with the part. You see, Larry Olivier actually wanted his wife Vivien Leigh to play the part of his second wife.' Laurence Olivier, for his part, commented: 'Without my success in *Rebecca* I would certainly never have become an international film star.'

Laurence Olivier in 1940 at the the time of the film, Rebecca. *He is reported to have said, 'Without my success in* Rebecca, *I would never have become an international film star.'*

During the production stages in Hollywood, Daphne was asked to go and oversee filming, but she declined and wrote to David Selznick, saying: 'I would prefer that the character of Rebecca is not shown in the film, as this would completely undo the plot.'

The film of *Rebecca* greatly pleased Daphne and she rated it the most successful adaptation of any of her books; she could not fault the casting at all.

Over the years television companies have also produced adaptations of some of du Maurier's most famous novels. It all began with the BBC television production in 1979 of *Rebecca*.

This was the first time that one of her stories had been filmed in actual Cornish locations, and the whole production benefited enormously.

Caerhays Castle was used as the fictional house, Manderley: the surrounding coastline was an excellent backdrop to the suspense and drama of the story. Daphne said about the series:

A rare photograph of Daphne du Maurier reading what is probably her most famous book

'When people watch this production of *Rebecca* they imagine I am sitting at home with a butler at my side, holding a silver tray, and here I am boiling an egg for my supper! On the whole, I thought the production quite good. Joanna David was really rather smashing, but again, I did think that the Hitchcock film was awfully well done and that takes some beating.' Many close friends of du Maurier thought that Joanna David bore a remarkable resemblance to the young Daphne.

When asked later about the success of this particular book, Daphne replied: 'I could never understand why it became so popular. I still get letters about the novel and this is why I published *The Rebecca Notebook*.' Even now, it remains a beautifully crafted and highly evocative novel. Tea on the lawn with the sound of the sea coming up from the shore; birds singing at dawn and rooks circling around the trees; the cottage in the cove; the lush rhododendrons and hydrangeas: these are only some of the images vividly described in her text which show her masterly talent for capturing mood and subtlety.

Frenchman's Creek

'When the East wind blows up Helford river'

Frenchman's Creek was first published in 1941; its romance and adventure immediately turned it into a highly popular novel. Ever since then it has been a well-loved title, read and enjoyed all over the world. Rightly, if somewhat pompously, did *The Sunday Times* predict: 'A heroine who is bound to make thousands of friends in spite of her somewhat questionable behaviour. It is set in and around the Helford River and you can find Frenchman's Creek on the map of Cornwall near Helford Village.' (Actually, you will find it marked on most maps as Frenchman's Pill, 'pill' being a dialect word for a creek.)

Fowey, Daphne du Maurier's home town and inspiration for so many of her novels

An evocative photograph of Frenchman's Creek, known locally as 'Frenchman's Pill': pill is the Cornish word for creek

Local people, though, are cautious about entering Frenchman's Creek, many of them believing it is 'spooked'. The truth is it has a genuinely haunted reputation in that an old man, taking a short cut across the creek, did not return home one night. In the morning they found him sitting upright in the river, dead, with his hat still on his head, and his long white beard running with water. In a strange way he lives on, in that his ghost is said to have appeared in local cottages and houses he knew in his lifetime.

As for the novel this is Daphne du Maurier at her Cornish best. She opens with the east wind blowing up Helford River when the

Joan Fontaine with Arturo de Cordova, who played the pirate opposite her Lady Dona

This photograph of Daphne, beside the boat in which she sailed to Frenchman's Creek on her honeymoon, was taken in 1965, shortly after her husband's death

Joan Fontaine with Basil Rathbone, who had been an early idol of Daphne during his London theatre days in the 1920s

Daphne introduced Martyn Shallcross, the author, to Joan Fontaine. Here he is interviewing Joan at the National Film Theatre in November 1978

waters become troubled and stirred – as too does the life of the heroine, beautiful Lady Dona, for while the gentry strive to capture a Frenchman, who plunders their coastline, Lady Dona finds excitement and passion through daring to love a pirate.

Among the bracken here on the cliffs above Lantivet Bay, east of Fowey, you can just see a tiny cottage, built originally perhaps for coastguards watching for smugglers.

During the early part of the Second World War, around 1941, Daphne worked here in secrecy, and this is where most of Frenchman's Creek was written. She also met her friend Christopher Puxley here for romantic picnics

A rare photograph of Daphne du Maurier with Joan Fontaine, star of Rebecca *and of* Frenchman's Creek. *It was taken outside Kilmarth in August 1978*

In the book there are many references to Philip Rashleigh who lived at Fowey. In one section Dona joins the French pirate in a raid on Fowey harbour where they capture Philip Rashleigh's boat and set out to sea in it. Daphne du Maurier had this to say about it: 'The story on the whole was largely imaginary. The house Navron was based on one of the old houses on the Helford River and this is the closest I have come to writing a romantic novel...'

The success of *Frenchman's Creek* resulted in the film rights soon being sold to America. Joan Fontaine was cast in the exciting role of Dona St Columb while Basil Rathbone and Reginald Denny were in the cast alongside Arturo de Cordova who played the pirate. Daphne told me, 'My husband loved the film because the music used on the sound track was *Clair de Lune*,' and Joan Fontaine told me, 'We couldn't film in Cornwall at the time because of the war, so we went to the north of California where you have inlets covered with trees growing down to the water's edge and actually it looks a lot like Cornwall.'

The King's General

'While the church clock at Tywardreath chimes the small hours, the only sound I hear is the sigh of the wind beneath my window and the murmur of the sea as the tide comes sweeping across the sands to the marshes below St Blazey bridge…'

Daphne liked to use real Cornish locations in her fictional stories. Sir Richard Grenvile, in The King's General, *was imprisoned at Launceston Castle. Towering above the roofs of the town, and a symbol of alien English power, it was known as 'Castle Terrible'.*

The Normans chose this location wisely, for the castle provided a good vantage point from which miles of landscape between Bodmin Moor and the great wilderness of Dartmoor could be watched and strategically controlled. During the Civil War Launceston Castle was repaired and it held out for a while against the Roundheads – until Cromwell's artillery shattered the fortifications and the garrison surrendered

Daphne du Maurier in August 1978, standing outside Kilmarth with one of her dogs, Ken. She had kept a dog since her childhood

The novels of Daphne du Maurier grew in a very definite fashion. She once explained: 'I have to think about it for months ... nothing on paper, just thoughts. Then I do a draft of notes; a skeleton if you like. I go through each chapter, and then re-read the book as a whole.'

The King's General she finished rapidly: a matter of just three months. She wrote it during the Second World War and reflected: 'I think the anxiety one feels in wartime helped me to write this book. My husband was abroad at the time and I think I caught the spirit of war in that book.' The novel is dedicated to her husband in rather an amusing way: 'To my husband, also a general, but, I trust, a more discreet one.' Sir Frederick Browning did, of course, enjoy a distinguished army career. A Commander of the British Airborne Corps, he won the DSO and later served as Treasurer to the Duke of Edinburgh. On retiring and settling in Cornwall, he became a member of Cornwall County Council.

The story of *The King's General* uses many splendid Cornish locations in the plot, and it is a tragedy that the novel never became a film. After Daphne du Maurier had completed it, Sir Alexander Korda sent a film crew down to Cornwall to film the author at work at Menabilly. Sadly when the film was due to go into production, Sir Alexander Korda, the producer, backed out for financial reasons, and the project fell through. In a conversation with Stewart Granger, he told me: 'The only story I was due to do of Daphne's was *The King's General*, and I was to have played the part of Sir Richard Grenvile.'

This, Daphne du Maurier's fifth novel, is set during the Civil War. It is a brilliant account of the love shared by Sir Richard Grenvile – the King's

Another Cornish fortress featuring in The King's General *is Pendennis, remembered for one of the longest sieges of the Civil War – five months. It was the last Royalist stronghold to fall, and its garrison was allowed to march out fully armed with banners flying, defeated by plague and starvation*

General in the West – and Honor Harris, as courageous as she was beautiful, during the war when Cornwall echoed to Royalist drums and rebel bugles. But this is more than a moving love story, for the novel underlines Dame Daphne's sense of history. She resurrects seventeenth-century Cornwall with great insight.

One episode relates to her own familiar neck of the Cornish woods – that narrow piece of land between Fowey and Par where the Parliamentary forces under the Earl of Essex fought a hopeless battle at Castle Dore, and the pages are peppered with historic locations spilling over into Devon, including Plymouth and Tavistock.

*Daphne du
Maurier in the
1960s, with
her daughter
Flavia and
grandchildren
outside
Menabilly*

But the heart and soul of the story is here in Cornwall: there are red crosses on the maps, marking the beaches where the invading troops should land (at Veryan, Pentewan and Crinnis); and beacons on the headlands (at The Nare, The Dodman and The Gribbin). There are also great Cornish families and individuals who feature strongly: the Arundells of Trerice, the Trelawnys of Trelawne, Sir Arthur Basset of Tehidy and Sir Charles Trevanion of Caerhays – although you will find different spellings of the people and places in the novel.

An intriguing postscript is that in 1824 Mr William Rashleigh of Menabilly had alterations made to the house and, in the process, masons uncovered a small room or cell. In it they found the skeleton of a young man seated on a stool dressed in the clothes of a Cavalier, as worn during the days of the Civil War. On consulting family records, William Rashleigh discovered that members of the Grenvile family had hidden at Menabilly before the rising of 1648. He surmised one had taken refuge in that secret room – and had been forgotten.

After *The King's General* the time spent on each novel increased significantly. The later titles took Daphne six to seven months. When actually engaged on a book, a regular work pattern emerged. Usually she wrote from 10.30 a.m. to 1 p.m. and from 5.30 to 7.30 p.m. Sometimes she worked for a while in the afternoon but, weather permitting, she normally went for walks.

September Tide

'Oh, well, if it blows like I think it will, the boat will drag. Something ought to be done about it. You never know what will happen with the September Tide.'

The play *September Tide* is, without doubt, one of Daphne's most famous Cornish tales. It was written during the 1940s and during its composition she realised the major character, Stella, would be ideal for the now middle-aged Gertrude Lawrence.

Lawrence was world famous as a musical comedy star and she had given Noel Coward many of his successes, with sparkling appearances in such shows as *Private Lives* and *Tonight at 8.30*.

Daphne had first met Lawrence at her father's home, Cannon Hall, in Hampstead during the 1930s. During this time Gerald du Maurier had starred in a play alongside her. It is an interesting quirk of fate that the du Maurier connection was later renewed when she made her big come-back to the London stage after the war in 1948 in *September Tide*. Gertie told Daphne: 'The part of the mother, Stella, is the role I could do something with. I could play it and I could make a success of it in London.'

Daphne told Michael Gough, who was also to appear in her play: 'When I write a story or a novel or a play, I am like a postman. I feel that I am delivering a letter, but a letter I do not want answered.'

The inspiration for *September Tide* is another Cornish location: both the Falmouth Estuary and the King Harry Ferry are integral to the story. Once again, she drew on personal experience, this time a meeting with Prince Philip before he was married to Princess Elizabeth. Prince Philip was introduced to Daphne by her husband, Boy Browning, who was then Comptroller of Buckingham Palace and an Aide to Prince Philip. She told me he seemed to be interested in the 'modern' marriage that Daphne and Boy Browning apparently had, with years of separation from each other, one living in London and the other in Cornwall.

Ferryside, Daphne's first Cornish home, also gave her inspiration for her play. After she went to live at Menabilly, Angela, her elder sister, resided at Ferryside alone, except for her dog. During those years, Angela was not a good sleeper and sometimes was awoken not only by her dog barking, but also by noises out in the harbour. On one occasion, the pilot for Fowey Harbour, Mr Mitchell, anchored his boat in the usual way outside the windows of Ferryside, thereby wakening the sleeping Angela. When she complained about the noise, the pilot suggested she leave a light on so they could see where she was and so cause the least amount of disturbance to her. The image of the light in the window was used by Daphne in *September Tide*.

Throughout her years in Cornwall, Daphne would often ride along the river and, on occasions, would visit her neighbour Leo Walmsley. He was an author whom she admired, not only because of his literary skills and his struggle against all the odds to write in difficult circumstances, but also because of his bohemian life style. He was often short of money so Daphne would offer him work at her house doing odd jobs. In fact, he built a wooden summer house for her at Menabilly.

Daphne rarely penned any congratulatory remarks in or about other people's books, but her esteem for Walmsley was such that praise for his work was spontaneous and warm. In 1954 she stated in a letter: 'I have been as long as a week with *The Golden Waterwheel* because I didn't want to finish it, and rationed myself to read it only at night. Alongside *Love in the Sun* and *Three Fevers* it's the best thing you've ever done.

'I know of no writer except you who can make the simple things of life become of so much importance to the reader. Somehow you combine great simplicity of style with tremendous narrative skill that is really dramatic, and your characters emerge warmly human and very lovable.'

Opposite: Daphne met Gertrude Lawrence in 1948 at the railway station when she arrived from America to play Stella. She took her to lunch, as her father would have done, at the Savoy Grill. When they were placed in a corner away from the public gaze, Gertie said, 'Let's go where people can see us!' This was the beginning of their long friendship

Almost as soon as her first book was published, Daphne became a successful novelist and author. As time went by this success spread worldwide, and it is perhaps no exaggeration to say she was the most famous author in the twentieth century to have lived and worked in Cornwall. However, the one medium she found the most difficult and the least enjoyable to work within was the play. Even though her father was a celebrated actor, the theatre had never really interested her. The attention her father had received from admirers backstage had only served to bring out her reclusive nature. Through her novels and books, she could live a life of total freedom, whether it was the girl in *Rebecca* or the girl in *Frenchman's Creek* or one of the characters in *My Cousin Rachel*. Each of them became part of her and, in many ways, an amalgam of her complicated and intriguing personality.

The fishing cove of Polkerris was always under the influence of the Rashleighs. Jonathan Rashleigh built this pier, in about 1750, to protect the fishing fleet, and the family also built the impressive pilchard cellars

Daphne was a chameleon-type figure whose multi-faceted qualities were used to great advantage in her literature. It is only in recent years that many facts surrounding her life and work have been brought to light. In many ways, *September Tide* is a good example. For years it was ignored as a rather inconsequential play, but because of the autobiographical elements in the plot and characters it is today enjoyed by a younger, but enthusiastic audience. Daphne had always intended only a few people would know the truth about *September Tide*. Now it is available for all her admirers and readers throughout the world.

My Cousin Rachel

'They used to hang men at Four Turnings in the old days...'

Speaking to *The Cornish Magazine* in 1963, Dame Daphne said: 'Each book has given me pleasure but, you know, when it's completed the whole thing fades. Each has its phase. What you want to write about changes with the years. *My Cousin Rachel* possibly marked the end of a phase... I cannot see myself settling down to another Cornish novel.'

Richard Burton with Olivia de Havilland in the film of My Cousin Rachel. *Part of the film was actually shot at St Dennis in Cornwall*

A 1947 photograph of Daphne with her children, Christian (nicknamed 'Kits'), Tessa and Flavia. Daphne told the author, 'I would sit on the beach doling out lemonade and sandwiches to the children, and no one would realise I was a bestselling author!'

Though *The House on the Strand* and *Rule Britannia* were yet to come, *My Cousin Rachel* was, in fact, the end of an era: her last truly historical novel set in Cornwall. *The House on the Strand* hovered between past and present, and *Rule Britannia* was set in the future. So *My Cousin Rachel* is an important volume in the du Maurier story.

First published in 1951, it has a *Jane Eyre* quality of suspense and ultimate tragedy. A reviewer for the magazine *Queen* referred to it as 'dramatic, surprising and masterly ... a highly skilled piece of storytelling.' Many of her readers might well vote this their favourite Cornish novel, for it is vintage du Maurier: mystery and murder mingling. The story opens with another memorable sentence: 'They used to hang men at Four Turnings in the old days.'

Ambrose married Rachel, Countess Sangalletti, in Italy and never returned home. His letters to his cousin Philip hinted that he was being poisoned, and when Philip arrives in Italy it is too late. Ambrose is already dead. Then Rachel crosses the English Channel; she comes to Cornwall and Philip finds himself torn between dark suspicion and passionate love. Is she a scheming murderess? Or is she the angelic woman she often seems?

The Rashleigh family name was used again as the fictional character's surname in the novel, although in the story the name was changed to 'Ashley'. Philip Ashley lived in a beautiful manor house in Cornwall, which had extensive grounds, full of rhododendron bushes. Daphne told me: 'So much of *Rachel* was imagined at my then home Menabilly; the idea for the sunken garden which would cause Rachel's death came to me one afternoon whilst out walking near Menabilly.'

Soon after the novel was published, the film rights were sold to America, and the possibilities for a great dramatic part for a slightly older actress were apparent. During the following month the celebrated film director George Cukor, well-known as a woman's director, came down to Cornwall and visited Daphne to discuss filming. He planned to use the enigmatic Swedish star, Greta Garbo, in the part of Rachel. This was to have been Garbo's return to the screen after an absence of several years. Unfortunately it was not to be and the film went on to be made

My Cousin Rachel came about after Daphne had visited Antony House in south-east Cornwall in about 1950. She liked to take a character from a well-known Cornish family and home, and here her choice was Rachel Carew around whom she created her story. It was a portrait of Rachel Carew which inspired her, and this still hangs in Antony House today. It was painted by Mary Beale, one of the first women professional painters. Rachel Carew, however, was not in the least like her counterpart in the novel. She married Ambrose Manaton of Kilworthy, and died young

with Richard Burton as Philip Ashley and Olivia de Havilland, Joan Fontaine's sister, as Rachel.

Daphne had this to say about the film: 'I never thought Olivia de Havilland quite the person I imagined as Rachel. I actually would have liked Vivien Leigh to have played the part; she told me in New York that she would love to play the part. She would have been splendid as Rachel.'

In 1983 BBC TV adapted *My Cousin Rachel*. Produced by Richard Beyon and directed by Brian Farnham, Geraldine Chaplin starred as Rachel. It made splendid television, and Geraldine Chaplin was an inspired choice for the part.

Throughout the novel the prose is typically Daphne du Maurier: clearcut and assured. The characters speak, act and react in such a way that we hurry from page to page. If this were the end of a Cornish innings, then Daphne du Maurier completed it with style – and story-telling brilliance.

Castle Dor

'It had no dimensions, small or great... what It was I could not say, the secret was beyond me.'

Castle Dor was a rare collaboration between a living author and a dead writer. It is a tale of nineteenth-century Cornwall, and is one of the saddest love stories the world has ever known.

The 'Tristan Stone' used to stand at the Four Turnings crossroads (cited in the first line of My Cousin Rachel*) but has been moved a little nearer to Fowey and a little further from Castle Dore, the legendary home of King Mark.*

It has a Latin inscription (now impossible to read) dating from about AD600: 'Drustan lies here, the son of Cunomorus'.

Drustan may have been the Tristan of legend. Cunomorus may have been Cynfawr, also known as Marcus Conomorus, who may have been King Mark. If so, then Tristan was having an affair with his stepmother...

The Haven, home of 'Q', Sir Arthur Quiller-Couch, who was one of Daphne's early friends and supporters at Fowey. His daughter, Foy, showed Daphne around the area in her gig which had many strange bells and bridle fastenings that made an enormous noise as they went by

'Q' was one of the great Cornish literary characters, author of many novels based on his beloved Fowey and first editor of The Oxford Book of English Verse. *Dining with him remained a vivid memory for Daphne du Maurier. She once said, 'It could be a bit frightening: in a way you sat on the edge of your chair. He was inclined to switch, broad-minded one moment and very rigid the next.' This portrait, by George Ellis, was taken on the eve of his 80th birthday in November 1943*

Foy Quiller-Couch, daughter of the celebrated Sir Arthur Quiller-Couch, explained how this book came about. She recalled how back in the 1920s she had ridden with her father up to Lantyan. The great man was already fascinated by the legend of Tristan and Iseult, and was enthusiastic about writing a book based on it, but setting the legend around the Fowey River.

However, it was a book and a theme for vacations. Sir Arthur was then at Cambridge and it was only in those precious holidays, back in Cornwall, that he was able to devote time and energy to his favourite project. Yet curiously, Foy Quiller-Couch expressed

The remains of Castle Dore (sometimes spelt Dor or even Dôr) stand in a field by the road linking Fowey and Lostwithiel. There is, frankly, nothing dramatic about the site today – all that remains is a large rough circle of banks and ditches. The romance of the place, which appealed to Daphne, was that when Castle Dore was excavated in the 1930s it was discovered that the fort had been reoccupied during the Dark Ages, the supposed time of King Arthur. Was this, then, truly the palace of King Mark?

the belief that her father somehow tired of the subject or, at least, felt the manuscript would never be good enough to publish. This upset her greatly but, interestingly, when Sir Arthur died in 1944 the unfinished manuscript came into her possession.

In a way it was a fortunate act because she then reversed her father's decision.

It was not, however, until 1959 when rereading the manuscript that she asked her friend Daphne du Maurier to complete it. She said: 'Daphne did it so brilliantly, weaving her words into his, that I believe no reader will know where and when the shuttle was transferred from my father's hand into hers.'

When Daphne du Maurier was interviewed, she confessed that her immediate reaction had been to say no, but that on reading the manuscript she, too, felt the spell and the magic of the story and therefore responded to the challenge. Moreover, she was under the very definite view that Doctor Carfax, a central character, was largely 'Q' himself.

This is Q's last novel or more accurately it is half Q's last novel: Dame Daphne took over the manuscript as it stood, which was somewhere about the halfway stage. Fortunately, Q had left a few substantial clues as to his ultimate intention. Though detection of the changeover may not be easy, readers who know their Daphne du Maurier will find greater pace and more sharply defined detail in the second half.

There is an interesting piece of literary replay in this collaboration between du Maurier and Q in that one of his earliest and most successful literary exploits was completing Robert Louis Stevenson's *St Ives*.

The genesis of *Castle Dor* is that soon after the 1914-18 war Q found 'Mark's Gate' on a local map and this discovery launched his search for place associations. In that search the idea of *Castle Dor* was born. In his imagination he brought together in a chance encounter Amyot, the Breton onion seller, and the beautiful and newly wed Linnet Lawherne. As the story unfolds the ancient legend takes command of reality, the principal characters finding their actions fatefully linked with the past.

The House on the Strand

'I was a happy tenant at Kilmarth' (Daphne du Maurier, 1981)

With her move from Menabilly in 1967 Daphne du Maurier now gave up real roots. The Rashleigh family wanted to move back to their ancestral home, and Daphne through the years had only been able to rent the estate, once reflecting: 'I could never buy the houses that I wanted...'

Kilmarth during the early 1980s on a spring morning. Daphne liked living at this, the dower house to Menabilly. Her husband had signed the lease just before his death

August 1978: Daphne and the author walking up to Kilmarth soon after a meeting with Joan Fontaine

With the death of her husband and the scattering of her family she found she was starting, almost to her disbelief, a new beginning. This new beginning took place a little further due west from Menabilly, at Kilmarth, the former dower house to Menabilly. It is a fine old house, built upon fourteenth-century foundations, that overlooks the great sweep of Par Bay. The name Kilmarth means in Cornish 'retreat of Mark'.

Once more a house began to interest Daphne; her imagination stirred images from the past and ideas gradually grew and developed into a new book.

The House on the Strand, which first saw the light of publication day in 1969, is a brilliant combination: part straight novel and part story of suspense. It has a wonderfully photographic quality, and as we travel from page to page, thanks to Daphne du Maurier's creativity and historical researches, we see Cornwall both in the twentieth and fourteenth centuries.

It is a fascinating plot: Dick Young, the central character, has been lent a house on the south coast of Cornwall, by a friend who is a professor of biophysics. He agrees to act as a guinea pig while he is there for a new drug which Professor Lane has discovered. The bottles await his arrival in the laboratory at Kilmarth. Little does he know that the prescribed dose is no less than a time machine, taking him back six hundred years to an earlier Cornish landscape.

On successive days Dick Young takes 'trips', always back to the same settings. Like an invisible man, he witnesses intrigue and adultery, even murder, but somehow he curiously feels himself personally involved. Hallucinations? Subconscious escape from his own life today? Or has Dick really travelled back in time?

This is Dame Daphne at her most beguiling. The reader feels impelled to rush along at express train speed towards the novel's

Daphne photographed in 1976 at the end of Kilmarth which faces Par Bay. With her are her dogs Ken and Mac who remained her companions until her death in 1989

final startling climax. Why this book has never reached the cinema screen must remain a literary and commercial mystery.

Robin Ellis, star of the *Poldark* series based on the bestselling novels of Winston Graham, took out an option on the story and planned to make a film of it in Cornwall. Daphne told me: 'Their ideas seemed to be so original, but I'm afraid the money just couldn't be raised to finance the film, which was a pity.'

Around this time Daphne was lucky enough to have one of her short stories turned into another memorable film, *Don't Look Now*, which was directed by the highly talented Nicolas Roeg. The film was a great success in Britain and throughout Europe. Set in Venice, the content slightly horrific, the film starred Julie Christie and Donald Sutherland. It was Donald Sutherland who told me: 'I loved the film. The story had a kind of Hitchcock feel of suspense, but I'm afraid it wasn't a great success in the States, which was a pity.'

Nevertheless *Don't Look Now* reawakened interest in Daphne's short stories. Often inspired by visits abroad, many of them contain horrific and psychic elements which make them totally different from her successful Cornish novels. Daphne told me, 'It is funny really, but the psychic element to my writing only shows itself in my short stories.'

This haunting quality of her short stories could be easily translated onto the screen to great effect. The fact that *The Birds* and *Don't Look Now* were made into outstanding films for the cinema underlines the very visual strength of her writing.

The fourteen stories that made up *The Rendezvous & Other Stories*, published by Gollancz in 1980, are a perfect example of her range and creativity. There is the case of the seemingly happily married woman who committed suicide in Paris for no apparent reason; an ambitious author plagued by women whom he has

The atmospheric ending of Nicolas Roeg's 1973 film of Don't Look Now, *which Daphne regarded as an excellent adaptation of her short story. She wrote to Nicolas Roeg, congratulating him and asking if he would film another of her stories*

used in his climb up the literary ladder; and a young man, who
finds he is destined to be disabled, trying to break the news to the
beautiful girl he had hoped to marry. Those are just three of her
varied themes. Interestingly, some of them were written before
her first novel was published.

In another collection, *Not After Midnight*, which was triggered
by her holiday in the Greek island of Crete, there are five 'long'
short stories that show how her settings could be as varied as her
plots: they cover Jerusalem and East Anglia, Venice and Ireland.

It was one of the most painful twists of reality in her personal
life story that her husband, who liked Kilmarth, died a few weeks
after signing the lease, and never lived there. Janet Watts, interviewing her for *The Observer* in 1981, asked her if the passage of
time had made widowhood easier to bear. Then, sixteen years
after her husband's death, she confessed, 'I don't know.'

Rule Britannia

'My last real Cornish novel' (Daphne du Maurier, 1982)

Daphne du Maurier's final chapter is *Rule Britannia* and it was inspired by her experience of living at Kilmarth.

This, her thirteenth novel, revolves around the character of Mad and an 'invasion' of Cornwall by the Americans. Mad is addicted to her home and says she would certainly die for it 'if I thought it would be any good'. One feels very strongly that those

When the author accompanied Daphne on a walk around Kilmarth, in 1976, she pointed out the locations for many of her famous stories, including this – Par Beach – for Rule Britannia. *Par Beach was where she liked to exercise her dogs every morning. She once told the author, 'When I first stopped writing, I did find it difficult to relax, because I had no hobbies – writing has always been my one and only interest'*

were the sentiments of the author, too. Thinking of Cornwall as almost an island, Daphne reflected her beliefs in the text as she justified the force of Mad's determination to defend her beloved Cornwall.

In *Rule Britannia* US marines land in Cornwall and Mad rallies friends, family and neighbours to protect their heritage. Emma lives with her grandmother, a distinguished and now retired actress. Mad is Emma's name for her grandmother. (The book is in fact dedicated to Gladys Cooper, a long-time friend.) Granddaughter and grandmother wake one morning to find their world shattered: there is no telephone and no radio, no post, but there is a warship in the bay with American troops advancing across the field in the direction of their home. From the moment she sees the Americans, Mad declares a kind of war on these interlopers.

The novel is meant to represent a time when Britain has withdrawn from the Common Market and, with the threat of bankruptcy, has decided that salvation lies in a union with the United States. In theory it is a partnership, although some have interpreted the story as a takeover bid.

This is, in fact, Daphne du Maurier at the height of her powers, drawing life-like characters with great perception. It is a wonderful finale in the true du Maurier tradition. As one of the jacket blurbs reflects: 'In Emma, looking at it all with clear young eyes, Daphne du Maurier has drawn one of her most enchanting heroines; and this engrossing book shows again what a versatile and perceptive writer she is.'

Vanishing Cornwall

'My Cornish autobiography' (Daphne du Maurier, 1981)

After her last novel, *Rule Britannia*, Daphne du Maurier continued to write, fascinated by the Elizabethan lives of 'the Bacon Boys'. The result was two more biographies, entitled *The Winding Stairs* and *The Golden Lads*. Of these two books she reflected: 'What interested me most when doing my Bacon research, I found that the maternal grandmother of Anthony and Francis Bacon had been Ann Fitzwilliam of Milton, near Peterborough, daughter of Sir William Fitzwilliam, friend of Wolsey and the first to live at Milton.'

Neither of these books achieved great success and the author sadly reflected: 'The trouble is, I'm afraid, the public see me essentially as a novelist and not a biographer.'

Daphne was fascinated by the half-Cornish Brontë family, and her work has often been compared with theirs. This house in Chapel Street, Penzance, was once the home of Maria Branwell, the mother of Charlotte, Emily, Anne and Branwell Brontë

One of the author's last photographs of himself and Dame Daphne, taken during April 1988

In looking at the life and times of this distinguished novelist one is tempted to ask, or at least, wonder: 'How much fiction was drawn from the well of personal experience and emotion?' She confessed there were always two lives to Daphne du Maurier: her marriage and the bringing up of two daughters and a son, and her writing self imagining someone else's life. On the subject of her own reading habits, Daphne always insisted, 'I never reopen my own work. Once it is finished that is it, I just put it away.'

In the early 1980s Daphne du Maurier's book *Vanishing Cornwall* was reissued with the original text and colour photographs taken by her son, Christian Browning. In a way it is her

Opposite: a sixteenth-century merchant's house in the heart of Fowey: the town was burnt down by the French in 1457, so few of its buildings are older than that

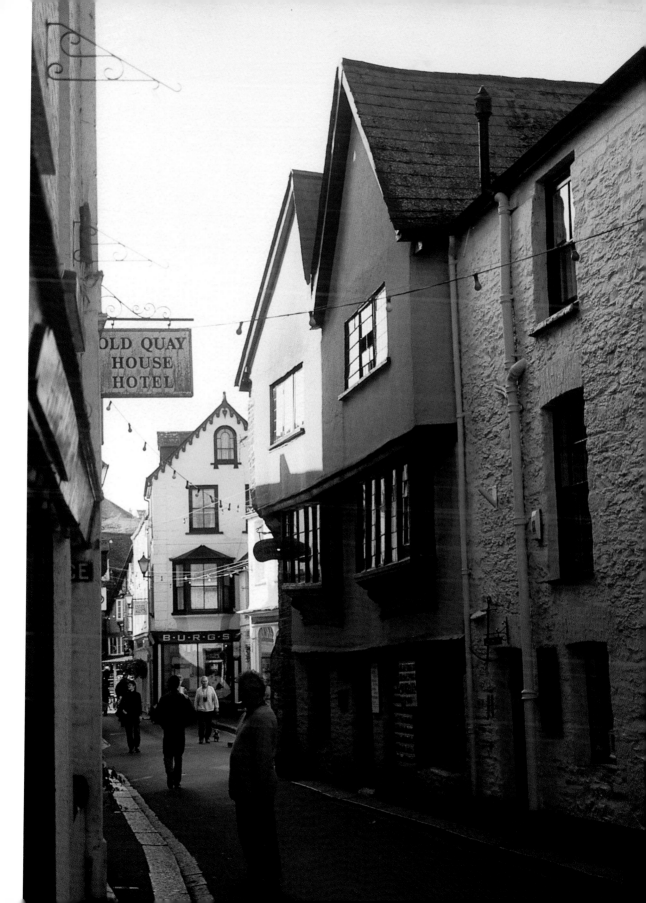

Inside Kilmarth in about 1985. Daphne felt the cold and would wear layers of jumpers, but even with failing health she tried to remain her charming self

tribute to Cornwall, containing chapters on the search for Arthur and for Tristan, the High Coast and The Lizard, and religion and superstition. Writing the original version at Menabilly in 1966 she dedicated it: 'To the memory of my husband because of memories shared and a mutual love of Cornwall; and to our son Christian, who photographed the present while I rambled on about the past.'

It remains a fine volume – as vivid and readable as any of her thirteen novels. In fact, in places the narrative is so colourful and dramatic that one is reminded of the truth of an ancient cliché – fact is truly stranger than fiction.

In the words of Tamsin Mitchell on Radio Cornwall, *Vanishing Cornwall* 'will stand as a lasting tribute to one woman's love of Cornwall for many years to come.'

Opposite: 'Ferryside', a recent view from the Fowey side of the ferry

The du Maurier legacy

'Do you think the dead come back and watch the living?'
Rebecca

'A hired car swept around the curve of the hill and suddenly the full expanse of Fowey Harbour was spread beneath us. The contrast of this sheet of white water, the nearby jetties, the moored ships, the grey roofs of Fowey across the way, the clustering cottages of Polruan on the opposite hill by the harbour mouth and narrow claustrophobic Looe where we had spent the night was astonishing. Like a gateway to another world. My spirits soared.'

That is how Dame Daphne opened a radio programme celebrating her eightieth birthday in 1987. Throughout her life she composed in a rich and diverse way, encompassing many types of writing: novels, non-fiction, short stories and plays. But it is her

handful of books set in Cornwall that have and will continue to assure her legendary status. In many ways her characters are extensions of the Cornish countryside; they were created by it and are therefore inseparable from the county she made her own.

Daphne has left a treasured legacy which is already cherished by her knowledgeable readers but which is also waiting to be discovered by new generations of admirers. Explore her work diligently and the rewards and insights into her life are great.

Daphne's insecurities and enigmatic character are particularly discernible in her novel *Rebecca*. During her life, Daphne told very few people the real reason for writing this, her most famous Cornish story. As a young woman, she felt jealous of her husband's previous girl friends, and was especially perturbed when she discovered a bundle of love letters written to her husband, Boy Browning, by his former fiancée, Jan Ricardo. Daphne used the character of Jan Ricardo, whom she knew to be tall, dark-haired and immaculately dressed, as the basis for her legendary Rebecca, the woman who was never seen by anyone but who continued to exert power throughout the drama.

Polridmouth beach, for ever associated with Rebecca *and the scuppering of her boat: in a sense, the second Mrs de Winter was* Daphne du Maurier

Both in her novels and in the films made from them, Daphne du Maurier's characters – each in a sense a part of her – live on. This is Joan Fontaine in Frenchman's Creek, *shot in Northern California in scenery not unlike Cornwall*

Daphne's love of places undeniably bordered on the obsessive, but it was something she was aware of – and it was certainly something she made use of in her work. Talking to Roy Plumley on the BBC radio programme *Desert Island Discs*, she explained how she first came to Menabilly:

'Well, there were my trespassing days. We walked a lot, my sisters and I, and we used to trespass around the grounds of Menabilly just the other side of the harbour from us at Fowey... This house wasn't lived in, because the owner lived away – he used to come down sometimes – and I got a terrific thing about this house, and eventually many years afterwards came to live there. I asked if I could possibly rent it during the war, and went to live there ... with the children (my husband was off in the war), from '43 till after he [Boy Browning] died in 1965.'

Later in the programme she admitted with enthusiasm: 'Oh, I have a terrific thing about the past.' She loved delving into history, and many of her books are also spiced with stories and images of the supernatural. She once told me: 'I've always wanted to see a ghost, you know. In fact, I joined the Ghost Club but in many ways, as I lived alone for many years, the thought of sharing my isolated home with a disturbed spirit rather frightened me.' In a

For the individuals lucky enough to know her, Daphne was not the recluse she was sometimes made out to be. Here are two of the author's favourite memories of her:

Daphne with the author outside the front entrance of Kilmarth in the Spring of 1982

1982, after lunch. Daphne's housekeeper, Esther Rowe, escorts the author's aunt Bernice to greet Daphne outside the long drawing room at Kilmarth. Daphne was always more than pleased to greet old friends

note to *Classics of the Macabre*, published shortly before her death, Daphne explained to her readers: 'I have always been fascinated by the unexplained, the darker side of life. I have a strong sense of the things that lie beyond our day-to-day perception and experience. It is, perhaps, an extension of this feeling that makes me live through the characters that I create.'

The lights are not dimmed at Manderley any more: they are shining bright. Mrs Danvers might be dead and Mary Yellan long forgotten, but Maxim de Winter is now forgiven for murdering his estranged wife. The ruined Manderley is still silent and secretive; nothing, even the passing years, can destroy these illusions. Daphne loved these invented characters dearly; they became a part of her. In fact, one afternoon she told me: 'I am the girl in *Rebecca*, you know. She had no name because I wrote in the first person. It was me, you know. That is why the public love that novel because there is more in that book about me than anything I have ever written; it should really have been entitled "An autobiography"'.

Daphne du Maurier was an intriguing writer: she was a spinner of webs, a creator of illusions, an innovative caster of spells. She was undeniably an artist: she could paint tellingly just as effectively as any painter. Time and time again, we are there, in the eye of her imagination.

The affection with which her work is held by the public can be compared with the following that such writers as Charlotte, Emily and Anne Brontë have generated. Fascination with their lives and work has grown over the years to such an extent that they have now achieved a legendary status. In the same way Daphne du Maurier, one of the most provocative and reclusive of English novelists, will continue to delight and enthrall generation upon generation of readers. Her vivid evocation of time, place and character captures our very being, just as Cornwall, land of beauty and mystery, always enchanted hers.

Opposite: the Fowey Hotel, always one of Daphne du Maurier's favourite places. On one occasion here, she pointed out to me landmarks around the harbour, including Punch's Cross where she and Angela used to swim as girls

Selected list of books and adaptations

The Loving Spirit (Heinemann, 1931)

I'll Never be Young Again (Heinemann, 1932)

The Progress of Julius (Heinemann, 1933)

Gerald: A Portrait (Gollancz, 1934)

Jamaica Inn (Gollancz, 1936)

The Du Mauriers (Gollancz, 1937)

Rebecca (Gollancz, 1938)

Come Wind, Come Weather (Heinemann, 1940)

Frenchman's Creek (Gollancz, 1941)

Hungry Hill (Gollancz, 1943)

The Years Between (Gollancz, 1945)

The King's General (Gollancz, 1946)

September Tide (Gollancz, 1949)

The Parasites (Gollancz, 1949)

The Young George du Maurier: A selection of his letters, 1860-1867 (ed)
   (Peter Davies, 1951)

My Cousin Rachel (Gollancz, 1951)

The Apple Tree (Gollancz, 1952)

Happy Christmas (Todd, 1953)

Mary Anne (Gollancz, 1954)

Early Stories (Todd, 1955)

The Scapegoat (Gollancz, 1957)

The Breaking Point (Gollancz, 1959)

The Infernal World of Branwell Brontë (Gollancz, 1960)

Castle Dor (JM Dent, 1962)

The Glass Blowers (Gollancz, 1963)

The Flight of the Falcon (Gollancz, 1965)

Vanishing Cornwall (Gollancz, 1967)

The House on the Strand (Gollancz, 1969)

Not After Midnight (Gollancz, 1971)

Rule Britannia (Gollancz, 1972)

Golden Lads: Anthony Bacon, Francis and the Friends (Gollancz, 1975)

The Winding Stair: Francis Bacon, his rise and fall (Gollancz, 1976)

Echoes from the Macabre (Gollancz, 1976)

Growing Pains: The shaping of a writer (Gollancz, 1977)

The Rendezvous and Other Stories (Gollancz, 1980)

The Rebecca Notebook and Other Memories (Gollancz, 1981)

Classics of the Macabre (Gollancz, 1987)

Films

Jamaica Inn (1939), directed by Alfred Hitchcock
  Cast: Charles Laughton, Maureen O'Hara, Leslie Banks, Robert
  Newton, Emlyn Williams, Wylie Watson, Marie Nay and Morland
  Graham

Rebecca (1940), directed by Alfred Hitchcock
  Cast: Joan Fontaine, Laurence Olivier, George Sanders, Judith
  Anderson, Reginald Denny, Nigel Bruce, Gladys Cooper, Florence
  Bates and C Aubrey Smith

Frenchman's Creek (1943), directed by Mitchell Leisen
  Cast: Joan Fontaine, Arturo de Cordova, Basil Rathbone, Nigel
  Bruce, Ralph Forbes, Cecil Kellaway and Moyna McGill

Hungry Hill (1945), directed by Brian Desmond Hurst
  Cast: Margaret Lockwood, Dennis Price, Cecil Parker, Michael
  Denison, F J McCormick, Dermot Walsh, Jean Simmons, Eileen
  Herlie, Eileen Crowe, and Barbara Waring

The Years Between (1947), directed by Compton Bennett
  Cast: Michael Redgrave, Valerie Hobson, Flora Robson, Felix
  Aylmer, Dulcie Gray, James McKechnie and Edward Rigby

My Cousin Rachel (1953), directed by Henry Koster
  Cast: Olivia de Havilland, Richard Burton, Audrey Dalton, John
  Sutton and Ronald Squire

The Scape Goat (1958), directed by Robert Hamer
  Cast: Alec Guinness, Bette Davis, Irene Worth, Nicole Maurey,
  Pamela Brown and Geoffrey Keen

The Birds (1963), directed by Alfred Hitchcock
  Cast: Tippi Hedren, Rod Taylor, Suzanne Pleshette, Jessica Tandy
  and Ethel Griffies

Don't Look Now (1973), directed by Nicolas Roeg
  Cast: Julie Christie, Donald Sutherland, Hilary Mason, Celia
  Matania and Massimo Serrato

Television series

Rebecca, screened in four parts during 1979 by the BBC
  Starring: Joanna David, Jeremy Brett and Anna Massey

My Cousin Rachel, screened in 1983 by the BBC
  Starring: Geraldine Chaplin

Jamaica Inn, screened in 1983 by Harlech Television
  Starring: Trevor Eve, Patrick McGoohan and Jane Seymour

Rebecca, screened in 1997 by Carlton Television
  Starring: Charles Dance, Emelia Fox, Diana Rigg and Faye Dunaway

Index